In 1940, folklorist Alan Lomax recorded Woody in a series of conversations and songs for the Library of Congress. Also during the 1940s, Woody recorded extensively for Moses Asch, founder of Folkways Records. The recordings from this period, which have been issued under the Smithsonian Folkways label, continue to be "touchstones" for young folk music singer/songwriters everywhere.

Woody Guthrie continued to write songs and perform with the Almanac Singers, the politically radical singing group of the late 1940s, some of whose members would later re-form as the Weavers, perhaps the most commercially successful and influential folk music group of the late 1940s and early 1950s. Managed by Harold Leventhal, a trusted friend and confidante, and supported by music publisher Howie Richmond, the Weavers helped to establish folk music as a viable commercial entity within the popular music industry.

Becoming increasingly restless and disillusioned with New York's radio and entertainment industry, Woody writes:

I got disgusted with the whole sissified and nervous rules of censorship on all my songs and ballads, and drove off down the road across the southern states again."

Leaving New York and traveling in his large newly-bought Plymouth, Woody received an invitation to go to Oregon where a documentary film project about the building of the Grand Coulee Dam sought to use his songwriting talent. The Bonneville Power Authority placed Woody on the federal payroll for a month and, here, he composed yet another remarkable collection of songs: *The Columbia River Songs*, which include Roll on Columbia and Grand Coulee Dam.

Despite Woody's constant traveling and performing during the 1940s, and with the final dissolution of his first marriage, Woody strenuously courted an already married young Martha Graham dancer named Marjorie Mazia. Woody and Marjorie were married in 1946. This relationship provided Woody a level of domestic stability and encouragement which he had previously not known, enabling him to complete and publish his first novel, ***Bound for Glory***, in 1943; a semi-autobiographical account of his Dust Bowl years, which generally received critical acclaim. Together, Woody and Marjorie had four children—Cathy, who died at age four in a tragic home accident, Arlo, Joady, and Nora.

Moved by his passion against Fascism, during World War II Woody served in both the Merchant Marine and the Army, shipping out to sea on several occasions with his buddies Cisco Houston and Jimmy Longhi. In one of many anti-Fascist songs written during the war, Woody tells us:

"We were seamen three,
Cisco, Jimmy and me;
Shipped out to beat the fascists
Across the land and sea."
Seamen Three

Throughout his tours of duty, as in civilian life, Woody's penchant for writing and drawing continued unabated. His capacity for creative self-expression seemed inexhaustible, whether on land or sea.

In 1946, Woody Guthrie, with his wife and children, returned to settle in Coney Island, New York. The peace he had fought so hard for seemed finally within his reach. It was during this time that Woody composed *Songs to Grow On*, a collection of children's songs which once again, gained him a great deal of success. However, soon thereafter, Woody's behavior and health began to deteriorate, becoming increasingly erratic and creating tensions in his personal and professional life. He left his family again, this time for California with his traveling protegé, Ramblin' Jack Elliott. In California, Woody remarried a third time, to a young woman named Anneke Van Kirk and had a daughter, Lorina Lynn.

Becoming more and more unpredictable during a final series of "road trips", Woody eventually returned to New York, where he was mistakenly diagnosed several times as suffering everything from alcoholism to schizophrenia. In fact, Woody suffered from Huntington's Chorea, the degenerative disease which would gradually and eventually rob him of all his health, talents, and abilities. This was the same disease which had forced his mother's institutionalization thirty years earlier.

In 1954, Woody admitted himself into Greystone Hospital in New Jersey, one of several that he would go in and out of for the next thirteen years. While at Creedmoor State Hospital in Queens, New York, Woody Guthrie died on October 3, 1967.

"Well, it's always we ramble, that river and I
All along your green valley, I'll work till I die
My land I'll defend with my life, if it be
Cause my pastures of plenty must always be free"

Pastures of Plenty

Having lived through some of the most significant historic movements and events of the Twentieth-Century—the Great Depression, the Great Dust Storm, World War II, the social and political upheavals resulting from Unionism, the Communist Party and the Cold War—Woody absorbed it all to become a prolific writer whose songs, ballads, prose and poetry captured the plight of "everyman." While traveling throughout the American landscape during the 1930s, 40s, and 50s, Woody's observations of what he saw and experienced has left for us a lasting and sometimes haunting legacy of images, sounds, ar voices of the marginalized, disenfranchised, and oppresse people with whom he struggled to survive despite all odc Although the corpus of original Woody Guthrie songs, or Woody preferred "people's songs," are, perhaps, his most re ognized contribution to American culture, the stinging ho esty, humor, and wit found even in his most vernacular pro writings exhibit Woody's fervent belief in social, political, ar spiritual justice.

Recognition of Woody Guthrie's work lives on. He has bee inducted into The Songwriters' Hall of Fame (1971), tl Nashville Songwriters Hall of Fame (1977), and The Rock ar Roll Hall of Fame and Museum (1988). He has received nume ous awards, including the U.S. Department of the Interio Conservation Award (1966), The Folk Alliance Lifetin Achievement Award (1996), and from the National Academ of Recording Arts and Scienc (1999). Colleges and univer ties such as Case Wester Reserve University have spo sored symposia and lecture Popular and folk musiciar such as Bruce Springsteen, Bil Bragg, Wilco, Ani DiFranc and countless others continu to draw inspiration fro Woody Guthrie, re-interpre ing and re-invigorating h songs for new audiences. Pe Seeger, Bob Dylan, Ar Guthrie, and Ramblin' Jac Elliot, are among the legions folk musicians, of every ag group, who are carrying the tradition of the harmonica ar guitar-playing singer/songwriter into the future. New bool and publications of Woody's words and drawings, even a ch dren's book, *This Land is Your Land* by folk artist Katl Jacobsen, have brought Guthrie back into the mainstream popular culture. The Smithsonian Institution and the Wooc Guthrie Foundation and Archives have collaborated on major traveling exhibition about Woody's life and legac allowing thousands of people to view for themselves Woody artwork, writings, and songs.

Clearly, Woody Guthrie's songs continue to speak to us ¿ about thoughts, ideas, and feelings which are as relevant ar meaningful today as when he lived them.

– Jorge Arevalo
Curator
Woody Guthrie Foundation and Archives

> **ALTHOUGH THE CORPUS OF ORIGINAL WOODY GUTHRIE SONGS, OR AS WOODY PREFERRED "PEOPLE'S SONGS," ARE, PERHAPS, HIS MOST RECOGNIZED CONTRIBUTION TO AMERICAN CULTURE, THE STINGING HONESTY, HUMOR, AND WIT FOUND EVEN IN HIS MOST VERNACULAR PROSE WRITINGS EXHIBIT WOODY'S FERVENT BELIEF IN SOCIAL, POLITICAL, AND SPIRITUAL JUSTICE.**

WOODY GUTHRIE
CLASSICS SONGBOOK
Songs written and recorded by Woody Guthrie

Edited by Judy Bell and Nora Guthrie
Original Illustrations by Woody Guthrie
Cover photo of Woody Guthrie by Robin Carson c. 1943
Cover and Biography pages designed by Tom Holmes
All artwork and photos courtesy of the Woody Guthrie Archives
©1994, 1999 and 2003 Ludlow Music, Inc., New York, NY
except for cover faux burlwood image ©1999 Pierre Finkelstein

Ludlow Music, Inc.

DISTRIBUTED BY

7777 W. BLUEMOUND RD. P.O. BOX 13819 MILWAUKEE, WI 53213

 The Richmond Organization

Woody Guthrie

Woodrow Wilson Guthrie was born on July 14, 1912, in Okemah, Oklahoma. Describing the small frontier town in Okfuskee County, Woody writes:

"Okemah was one of the singingest, square dancingest, drinkingest, yellingest, preachingest, walkingest, talkingest, laughingest, cryingest, shootingest, fistfightingest, bleedingest, gamblingest, gun, club, and razor carryingest of our ranch towns and farm towns, because it blossomed out into one of our first Oil Boom Towns."

Woody was the second-born son to Charles and Nora Guthrie. His father was a cowboy, land speculator, and local politician. His Kansas-born mother profoundly influenced Woody in ways which would become apparent as he grew older. Slightly built, with an extremely full and curly head of hair, Woody was both a precocious and unconventional boy from the start. A keen observer of the world around him, during his early years in Oklahoma, Woody experienced the first in a series of tragic personal losses which would haunt him throughout his life. The death of his older sister Clara, his father's financial and physical ruin, and the institutionalization of his mother, devastated Woody's family and home, forming a uniquely wry and rambling outlook on life.

In 1931, when Okemah's boomtown period went bust, Woody left for Texas. In the panhandle town of Pampa, he fell in love and married Mary Jennings in 1933, the younger sister of a friend and musician named Matt Jennings. Together, Woody and Mary had three children, Gwen, Sue, and Bill. It was with Matt Jennings and Cluster Baker that Woody made his first attempt at a music "career," forming The Corn Cob Trio. However, if the Great Depression made it hard to support his family, the Great Dust Storm which hit the Great Plains in 1935, made it impossible. Due to the lack of work, and driven by a search for a better life, Woody headed west along with the mass migration of "dust bowl refugees" known as "Okies." These farmers and unemployed workers from Oklahoma, Kansas, Tennessee, and Georgia had also lost their homes and land, and so set out with their families in search of opportuni- ties elsewhere. Moneyless and hungry, Woody hitchhiked rode freight trains, and even walked to California, developing a love for traveling on the "open road"—a practice which h would repeat often.

By the time he arrived in California, in 1937, Woody had experienced the intense scorn, hatred, and antagonism of resident Californians who were opposed to the influx of "outsiders." Woody's identification with "outsider" status would become part and parcel of his political and social positioning, on which gradually worked its way into his songwriting, a evinced in his *Dust Bowl Ballads* such as I Ain't Got No Home Goin' Down the Road Feelin' Bad, Talking Dust Bowl Blues, To Joad and Hard Travelin'. His 1937 radio broadcasts on KFVL Los Angeles, and XELO (just over the border in Mexico brought Woody and his new singing partner, Maxine "Left Lou" Crissman wide public attention, while providing hir with a forum from which he could develop his talent for con troversial social commentary and criticism on topics rangin from corrupt politicians, lawyers, and businessmen to praisin the humanist principles of Jesus Christ, Pretty Boy Floyd, an Union organizers.

Never one to become comfortable with success, or being i one place for too long, in 1939 Woody headed east for Ne York City, where he was embraced for his Steinbeckian home spun wisdom and musical "authenticity" by leftist organiza tions, artists, writers, musicians, and other intellectuals.

"..I sang at a hundred IWO [International Workers' Order] lodges and met every color and kind of human being you can imagine."

Lead Belly, Cisco Houston, Burl Ives, Pete Seeger, Will Gee Sonny Terry, Brownie McGhee, Josh White, Millard Lampel Bess Hawes, Sis Cunningham, among many others, becam Woody's friends and collaborators, taking up such social cau es as Union organizing, anti-Fascism, strengthening th Communist Party, and generally fighting for the things the believed in the only way they knew how, through politica songs of protest.

This Land Is Your Land

Words and Music by
WOODY GUTHRIE

With spirit

CHORUS

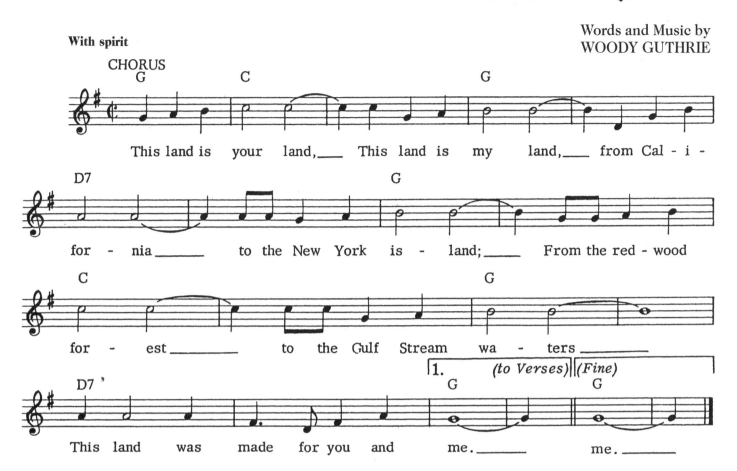

As I was walking that ribbon of highway,
I saw above me that endless skyway:
I saw below me that golden valley:
This land was made for you and me.

I've roamed and rambled and I followed my footsteps
To the sparkling sands of her diamond deserts;
And all around me a voice was sounding:
This land was made for you and me.

When the sun came shining, and I was strolling,
And the wheat fields waving and the dust clouds rolling,
As the fog was lifting a voice was chanting:
This land was made for you and me.

As I went walking, I saw a sign there,
And on the sign it said "No Trespassing."
But on the other side it didn't say nothing,
That side was made for you and me.

In the shadow of the steeple I saw my people,
By the relief office I seen my people;
As they stood there hungry, I stood there asking
Is this land made for you and me?

Nobody living can ever stop me,
As I go walking that freedom highway;
Nobody living can ever make me turn back,
This land was made for you and me.

So Long it's Been Good To Know Yuh

Dust Bowl Ballad

(Dusty Old Dust)

Words and Music by
WOODY GUTHRIE

Rollicking country waltz

Verse:

1. I've sung this song, but I'll sing it ___ a - gain, Of the
I've sung this song, but I'll sing it ___ a - gain, Of the

place that I lived on the wild, wind - y plains. In the month called
peo - ple I've met and the plac - es I've been. Of ___ some of the

A - pril, the coun-ty ___ called Gray, And here's what all of the
trou - bles that both-ered ___ my mind, And a lot of good peo - ple that

Chorus:

peo - ple there say:
I've left be - hind, say - ing:
So long, it's been good to know ye,

So long, it's been good to know ye, So long, it's

been good to know ye, This dust - y old dust is a - get - ting ___ my
(pop. version) What a long time ___ since I've ___ been

home, _____ and I've got to be drift - ing a - long. _____
home, _____

Dust Bowl Version
A dust storm hit, and it hit like thunder;
It dustedus over and it covered us under;
Blocked out the traffic and blocked out the sun.
Straight for home all the people did run. (Chorus)

We talked of the end of the world, and then
We'd sing a song, and then sing it again;
We'd sit for an hour and not say a word,
And then these words would be heard: (Chours)

The sweethearts sat in the dark and they sparked.
They hugged and kissed in that dusty old dark.
They sighed and cried, hugged and kissed,
Instead of marriage they talked like this: Honey (Chorus)

Now, the telephone rang and it jumped off the wall;
That was the preacher a-making his call.
He said, "Kind friend, this may be the end;
You've got your last chance of salvation of sin."
(Sing verses consecutively)

The churches was jammed, and the churches was packed,
And that dusty old dust storm blowed so black;
The preacher could not read a word of his text;
And he folded his specs and he took up collection, said: (Chorus)

Popular Version / hit record by the Weavers, 1951
The sweethearts sat in the dark and they sparked,
They hugged and kissed in that dusty old dark,
They sighed and cried, hugged and kissed,
Instead of marriage they talked like this: Honey (Chorus)

I went to your fam'ly and asked them for you.
They all said, "Take her, oh, take her, please do!
She can't cook or sew and she won't scrub your floor,"
So I put on my hat and tiptoed out the door, saying: (Shorus)

I walked down the street to the grocery store.
It was crowed with people both rich and both poor.
I asked the man how his butter was sold;
He said, "One pound of butter for two pounds of gold." I said: (Chorus)

My telephone rang and it jumped off the wall.
That was the preacher a'making a call.
He said, "We're waitin' to tie the knot;
You're gettin' married, believe it or not!"
(Sing verses consecutively)

The church it was jammed, the church it was packed;
The pews were so crowded from front to the back.
A thousand friends waited to kiss my new bride,
But I was so anxious I rushed her outside. Told them: (Chorus)

Pastures of Plenty

Dust Bowl Ballad

Words and Music by
WOODY GUTHRIE

Moderately

It's a might-y hard row that my poor hands have hoed;

My poor feet have trav-eled a hot dust-y road.

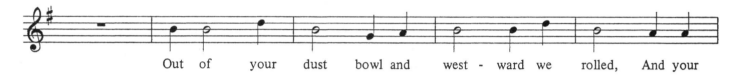

Out of your dust bowl and west-ward we rolled, And your

des-ert was hot and your moun-tains were cold.

I worked in your orchards of peaches and prunes,
Slept on the ground in the light of your moon,
On the edge of your city you've seen us and then,
We come with the dust and we go with the wind.

California and Arizona, I make all your crops,
And it's north up to Oregon to gather your hops,
Dig the beets from your ground, cut the grapes from your vines,
To set on your table your light sparkling wine.

Green pastures of plenty from dry desert ground,
From that Grand Coulee Dam where the water runs down,
Every state in this union us migrants have been,
We work in this fight, and we'll fight till we win.

Well, it's always we ramble, that river and I,
All along your green valley I'll work till I die,
My land I'll defend with my life, if it be,
'Cause my pastures of plenty must always be free.

Words by
WOODY GUTHRIE

Deportee *
(Plane Wreck at Los Gatos)

Music by
MARTIN HOFFMAN

Moderately

The crops are all in and the peach-es are rot-t'ning.

The or-an-ges piled in their cre-o-sote dumps.

You're fly-ing 'em back to the Mex-i-can bor-der, To

pay all their mon-ey to wade back a-gain. Good-

bye to my Juan, good-bye, Ro-sa-li-ta, A-

dios mis a-mi-gos, Je-sus y Ma-ri-a; You

won't have your names when you ride the big air-plane,

All they will call you will be de-por-tees.

* Jan. 28, 1948, Fresno, CA

My father's own father, he waded that river,
They took all the money he made in his life;
My brothers and sisters come working the fruit trees,
And they rode the truck till they took down and died.

Some of us are illegal, and some are not wanted,
Our work contract's out and we have to move on;
Six hundred miles to that Mexican border,
They chase us like outlaws, like rustlers, like thieves.

We died in your hills, we died in your deserts,
We died in your valleys and died on your plains,
We died 'neath your trees and we died in your bushes,
Both sides of the river, we died just the same.

The sky plane caught fire over Los Gatos canyon,
A fireball of lightning, and shook all our hills,
Who are all these friends, all scattered like dry leaves?
The radio says they are just deportees.

Is this the best way we can grow our big orchards?
Is this the best way we can grow our good fruit?
To fall like dry leaves to rot on my topsoil
And be called by no name except deportees?

Do Re Mi

Dust Bowl Ballad

Words and Music by
WOODY GUTHRIE

Lots of folks back east, they say, leav-in' home ev-'ry day, Beat-in' the hot old dus-ty way_ to the Cal-i-for-nia line. 'Cross the des-ert sands they roll, get-ting out_ of that old dust bowl, they think they're go-ing to a su-gar bowl_ but here is what they find: Now the po-lice at the port of en-try say, "You're num-ber four-teen thou-sand for to-day."

Chorus:
Oh, if you ain't got the do-re-mi, folks, if you ain't got the do-re-mi,_ Why, you bet-ter go back_ to beau-ti-ful Tex-as,_ Ok-la-ho-ma, Kan-sas,

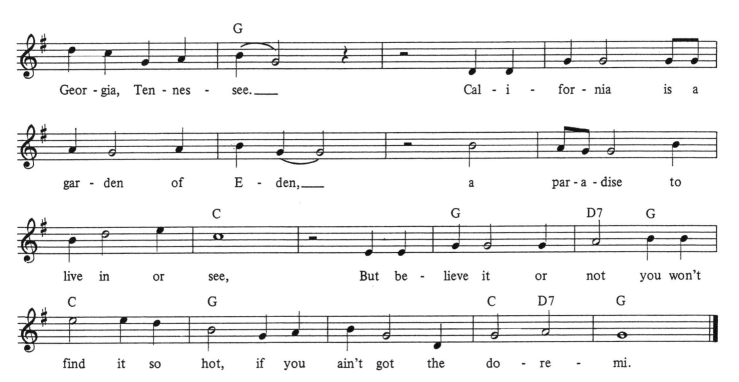

Geor - gia, Ten - nes - see.___ Cal - i - for - nia is a

gar - den of E - den,___ a par - a - dise to

live in or see, But be - lieve it or not you won't

find it so hot, if you ain't got the do - re - mi.

WE PLEGE OUR ALEGIANCE TO OUR FLAG ...... AN TO WALL ST., FOR WHICH IT STANDS ..... ONE DOLLAR, UNGETTABLE .....

If you want to buy you a home or farm
That can't do nobody harm,
Or take your vacation by the mountains or sea,
Don't swap your old cow for a car,
You'd better stay right where you are;
You'd better take this little tip from me.
'Cause I look through the want ads every day,
But the headlines on the papers always say:
(Chorus)

OKLAHOMA HILLS

Words and Music by
WOODY GUTHRIE AND JACK GUTHRIE

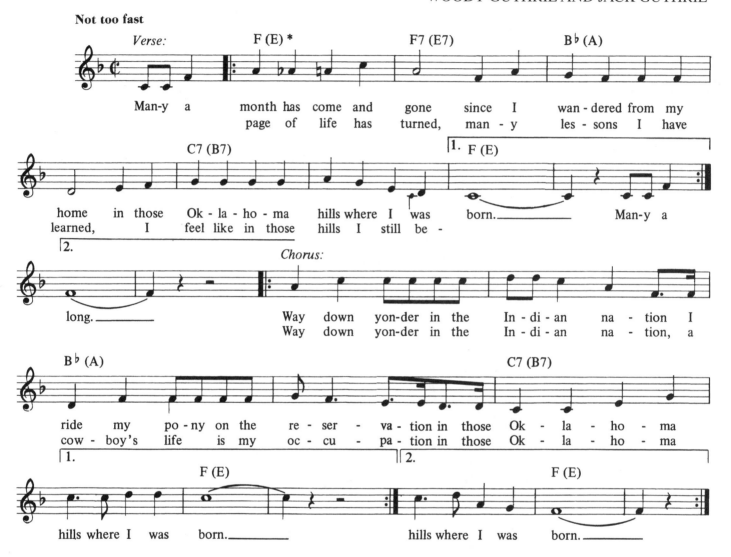

Not too fast

Verse:

Man-y a month has come and gone since I wan-dered from my
page of life has turned, since man-y les-sons I have

home in those Ok-la-ho-ma hills where I was born._____ Man-y a
learned, I feel like in those hills I still be-

long._____

Chorus:

Way down yon-der in the In-di-an na-tion I
Way down yon-der in the In-di-an na-tion, a

ride my po-ny on the re-ser-va-tion in those Ok-la-ho-ma
cow-boy's life is my oc-cu-pa-tion in those Ok-la-ho-ma

hills where I was born._____

hills where I was born._____

* Chord symbols in parentheses for guitar with capo on 1st fret.

But as I sit here today, many miles I am away
From the place I rode my pony through the draw,
Where the oak and blackjack trees kiss the playful prairie breeze
In those Oklahoma hills where I was born. (Chorus)

Now as I turn life a page to a land of great osage
In those Oklahoma hills where I was born,
Where the black oil rolls and flows and the snow-white cotton grows
In those Oklahoma hills where I was born. (Chorus)

© 1945 (Renewed) Unichappell Music Inc., Michael H. Goldsen, Inc. and Woody Guthrie Publications, Inc.
All Rights for Woody Guthrie Publications, Inc. Administered by BMG Rights Management (US) LLC
All Rights Reserved   Used by Permission

Roll On, Columbia

Columbia River Collection Bonneville Power Authority, 1941

Words by
WOODY GUTHRIE

Music Based on "Goodnight, Irene"
HUDDIE LEDBETTER and JOHN LOMAX

Moderately, in one

Roll on, Columbia, roll on. Roll on, Columbia, roll on. Your power is turning our darkness to dawn, So, roll on, Columbia, roll on!

Green Douglas firs where the waters cut through. Down her wild mountains and canyons she flew. Canadian Northwest to the oceans so blue, Roll on, Columbia, roll on!

Other great rivers add power to you,
Yakima, Snake and the Klickitat too,
Sandy Willamette and Hood River too,
Roll on, Columbia, roll on.

Tom Jefferson's vision would not let him rest,
An empire he saw in the Pacific Northwest.
Sent Lewis and Clark and they did the rest,
Roll on, Columbia, roll on (Chorus)

It's there on your banks that we fought many a fight,
Sheridan's boys in the blockhouse that night,
They saw us in death but never in flight,
Roll on, Columbia, roll on (Chorus)

At Bonneville now there are ships in the locks,
The waters have risen and cleared all the rocks,
Shiploads of plenty will steam past the docks,
So roll on, Columbia, roll on.

And on up the river is Grand Coulee Dam,
The mightiest thing ever built by a man,
To run the great factories and water the land,
It's roll on, Columbia, roll on.

These mighty men labored by day and by night,
Matching their strength 'gainst the river's wild flight,
Through rapids and falls they won the hard fight,
Roll on, Columbia, roll on.

Vigilante Man

Words and Music by
WOODY GUTHRIE

Dust Bowl Ballad

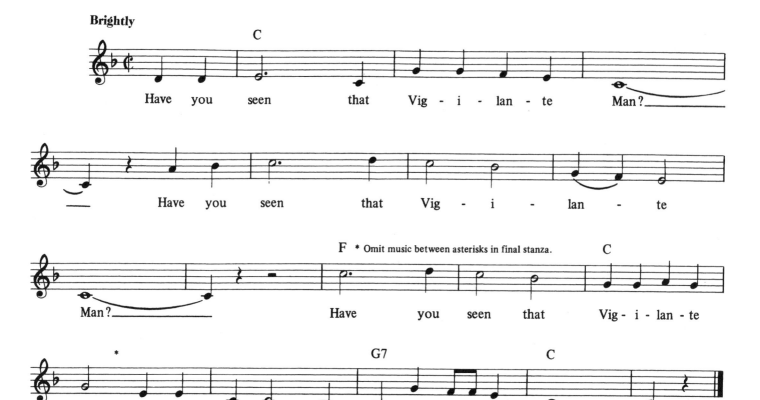

Well, what is a Vigilante Man?
Tell me what is a Vigilante Man?
Has he got a club in his hand?
Is that a Vigilante Man?

Rainy night down in the engine house,
Sleeping just as still as a mouse,
Man come along and chased us out in the rain,
Was that a Vigilante Man?

Stormy days we'd pass the time away
Sleeping in some good warm place,
A cop come along and we give him a little race,
Say, was that a Vigilante Man?

Preacher Casey was just a working man,
And he said, unite all us working men,
They killed him in the river, some strange man,
Was that your Vigilante Man?

Oh, why does a Vigilante Man
Oh, why does a Vigilante Man
Carry that sawed off shotgun in his hand?
Would he shoot his brother and sister down?

I rambled around from town to town,
I rambled around from town to town,
And they herded us around like a wild herd of cattle,
Was that your Vigilante Man?

Have you seen that Vigilante Man?
Have you seen that Vigilante Man?
I've heard his name all over the land.

THIS TRAIN IS BOUND FOR GLORY

New Words and Music Adaptation by
WOODY GUTHRIE

Moderately, in two

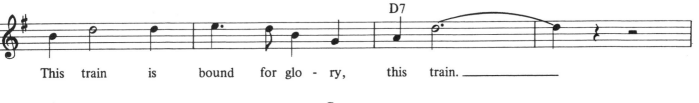

G
This train is bound for glo - ry, this train,_____

D7
This train is bound for glo - ry, this train._____

G   C
This train is bound for glo - ry, don't car-ry noth-ing but the right-eous and the ho - ly,

G
This train is bound for glo - ry, this train!_____

This train don't carry no gamblers, this train; (2)
This train don't carry no gamblers,
Liars, thieves nor big shot ramblers,
This train is bound for glory, this train.

This train don't carry no liars, this train; (2)
This train don't carry no liars,
She's streamlined and a midnight flyer,
This train don't carry no liars, this train.

This train don't carry no smokers, this train; (2)
This train don't carry no smokers,
Two-bit liars, small-time jokers,
This train don't carry no smokers, this train.

This train don't carry no con men, this train; (2)
This train don't carry no con men,
No wheeler-dealers, here and gone men,
This train don't carry no con men, this train.

This train don't carry no rustlers, this train; (2)
This train don't carry no rustlers,
Sidestreet walkers, two-bit hustlers,
This train is bound for glory, this train.

Biggest Thing That Man Has Ever Done

(The Great Historical Bum)

Words and Music by
WOODY GUTHRIE

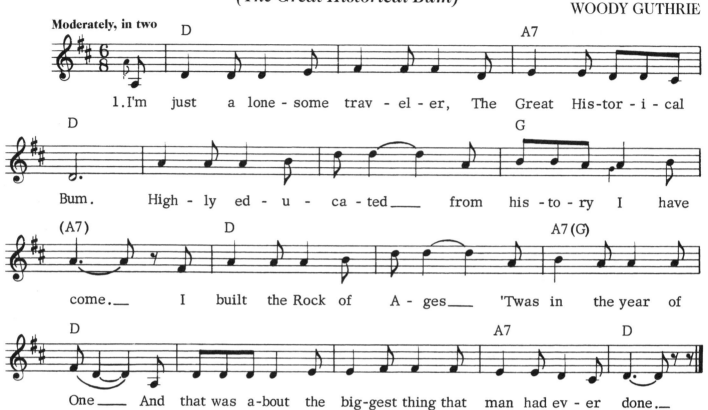

Moderately, in two

1.I'm just a lone-some trav-el-er, The Great His-tor-i-cal Bum. High-ly ed-u-ca-ted___ from his-to-ry I have come.___ I built the Rock of A-ges___ 'Twas in the year of One___ And that was a-bout the big-gest thing that man had ev-er done.___

OLD POLITICAL MACHINERY

"ALL THINGS ARE
TRANSIENT, FLEETING,
AND DESTINED TO PASS
AWAY" _____ "BUDDHA".

I worked in the Garden of Eden, that was the year of Two
Joined the apple picker's union, I always paid my dues;
I'm the man that signed the contract to raise the rising sun,
And that was about the biggest thing that man had ever done.

I was straw boss on the Pyramids, the Tower of Babel, too;
I opened up the ocean, let the migrant children through;
I fought a million battles and I never lost a one,
And that was about the biggest thing that man had ever done.

I beat the daring Roman. I beat the daring Turk;
Defeated Nero's Army with thirty minutes' work;
I stopped the mighty Kaiser. I stopped the mighty Hun;
And that was about the biggest thing that man has ever done.

I was in the Revolution when we set this country free;
It was me and a couple of Indians that dumped the Boston Tea;
We won the battle at Valley Forge and Battle of Bully Run;
And that was about the biggest thing that man has ever done.

Next we won the Slavery War, some other folks and me;
I beat the chains from off their legs and set my people free;
The Slavery men they lost the war, and Freedom's men had won;
And that was about the biggest thing that man had ever done.

Next I took to farming on the great midwestern plain;
The dust it blowed a hundred years, it never come a rain;
Me and a million other folks we left there on the run;
And that was about the biggest thing that man has ever done.

I clumb these rocky canyons where the Columbia River rolls;
Seen the salmon leaping the rapids and the falls;
'Twas there I built my Coulee Dam in the state of Washington;
And that was about the biggest thing that man has done.

Three times the size of Boulder Dam or the highest Pyramid;
It makes the Tower of Babel a plaything for the kids;
From the rising of the river to the setting of the sun,
My Coulee Dam's the biggest thing that man has ever done.

There's man acrost this ocean, and I guess you know him well;
His name is Adolf Hitler, god damn his soul to hell;
We'll kick him in the panzers and we'll put him on the run;
And this will be the biggest thing that man has ever done.

There's warehouse guys and teamsters and guys that skin the cats,
Guys that run my steel mill, my furnace, and my blast;
We'll stop these Axis rattlesnakes and thieves of old Nippon;
And that will be the biggest thing that man has ever done.

I better quit my talking 'cause I told you all I know;
But please remember, pardner, wherever you may go;
The people are building a peaceful world, and when the job is done,
That'll be the biggest thing that man has ever done.

Union Maid

Words and Music by
WOODY GUTHRIE
(Melody based on a traditional theme)

With spirit

This union maid was wise to the tricks of company spies:
She never got fooled by a company stool, she'd always organize the guys;
She always got her way when she struck for higher pay;
She'd show her card to the company guard and this is what she'd say: (Chorus)

You gals who want to be free, just take a little tip from me:
Get you a man who's a union man and join the Ladies' Auxiliary;
Married life ain't hard when you've got a union card,
A union man has a happy life when he's got a union wife. (Chorus)

1913 Massacre

Words and Music by
WOODY GUTHRIE

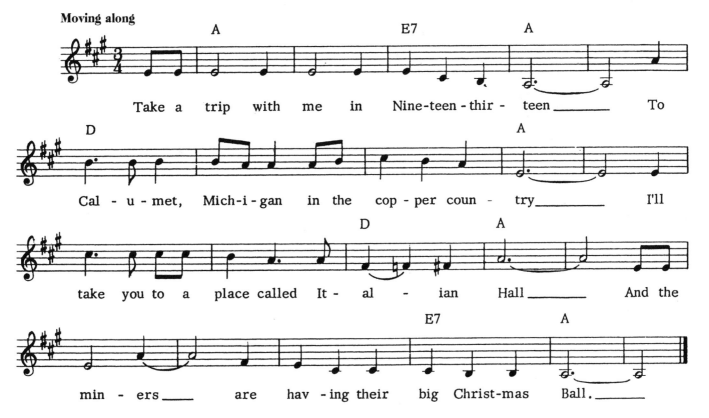

Moving along

Take a trip with me in Nine-teen-thir-teen _____ To Cal-u-met, Mich-i-gan in the cop-per coun-try_____ I'll take you to a place called It-al-ian Hall _____ And the min-ers___ are hav-ing their big Christ-mas Ball. _____

UNION/LABOR

I'll take you in a door and up a high stairs,
Singing and dancing is heard everywheres.
I'll let you shake hands with the people you see
And watch the kids dance 'round the big Christmas tree.

There's talking and laughing and songs in the air,
And the spirit of Christmas is there everywhere.
Before you know it you're friends with us all,
And you're dancing around and around in the hall.

You ask about work and you ask about pay;
They'll tell you they make less than a dollar a day,
Working their copper claims, risking their lives.
So it's fun to spend Christmas with children and wives.

A little girl sits down by the Christmas tree lights
To play the piano so you gotta keep quiet.
To hear all this fun you would not realize
That the copper boss thug men are milling outside.

The copper boss thugs stuck their heads in the door;
One of them yelled and he screamed, "There's a fire."
A lady she hollered, "There's no such a thing;
Keep on with your party, there's no such a thing."

A few people rushed and there's only a few;
"It's just the thugs and the scabs fooling you."
A man grabbed his daughter and he carried her down,
But the thugs held the door and they could not get out.

And then others followed, a hundred or more,
But most everybody remained on the floor.
The gun thugs, they laughed at their murderous joke,
And the children were smothered on the stairs by the door.

Such a terrible sight I never did see;
We carried our children back up to their tree.
The scabs outside still laughed at their spree,
And the children that died there was seventy-three.

The piano played a slow funeral tune,
And the town was lit up by a cold Christmas moon.
The parents, they cried and the miners, they moaned,
"See what your greed for money has done?"

JACKHAMMER JOHN

" I wrote my first Jackhammer Blues when I was a livin' in a little old hotel up in New York Town, and the boys was a takin' up the pavement just below my window; but here it is set to a little faster time, and cut in one of the farthest, youngest, hardest working countries you ever seen, in the rough and tumble valley of the big Columbia River, out here in the good old Pacific Northwest, Oregon".

Woody Guthrie - This song written May 12, 1941

Words and New Music Adaptation by
WOODY GUTHRIE

I was borned in Portland town,
Built every port from Alasky down; (Refrain)
Built your bridges, dug your mines,
Been in jail a thousand times. (Refrain)

Jackhammer, jackhammer, where you been?
Been out a-chasin' them gals again...
Jackhammer man from a jackhammer town,
I can hammer on a hammer till the sun goes down...

I hammered on the boulder, hammered on the butte,
Columbia River on a five-mile chute...
Workin' on the Bonneville, hammered all night
A-tryin' to bring the people some electric light...

I hammered on Bonneville, Coulee too,
Always broke when my job was through...
I hammered on the river from sun to sun,
Fifteen million salmon run...

I hammered in the rain, I hammered in the dust,
I hammered in the best and I hammered in the worst...
I got a jackhammer gal just as sweet as pie,
And I'm a-gonna hammer till the day I die...

The Grand Coulee Dam

Columbia River Collection
Bonneville Power Authority, 1941

Words and Music by
WOODY GUTHRIE
(Melody based on a traditional theme)

Moderately, in two

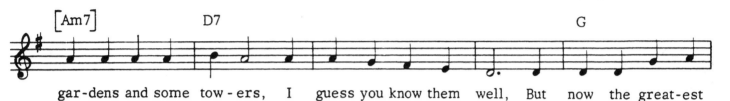

Well, the world has sev-en won-ders that the trav-'lers al-ways tell, Some

gar-dens and some tow-ers, I guess you know them well, But now the great-est

won-der is in Un-cle Sam's fair land, It's the big Co-lum-bia Riv-er and the

1.
big Grand Cou-lee Dam. 2.She heads big Grand Cou-lee Dam.

Last time

UNION/LABOR

She heads up the Canadian Rockies where the rippling waters glide,
Comes a-roaring down the canyon to meet the salty tide,
Of the wide Pacific Ocean where the sun sets in the West
And the big Grand Coulee country in the land I love the best.

In the misty crystal glitter of that wild and wind ward spray,
Men have fought the pounding waters and met a watery grave,
Well, she tore their boats to splinters but she gave men dreams to dream
Of the day the Coulee Dam would cross that wild and wasted stream.

Uncle Sam took up the challenge in the year of 'thirty-three,
For the farmer and the factory and all of you and me,
He said, "Roll along, Columbia, you can ramble to the sea,
But river, while you're rambling, you can do some work for me."

Now in Washington and Oregon you can hear the factories hum,
Making chrome and making manganese and light aluminum,
And there roars the flying fortress now to fight for Uncle Sam,
Spawned upon the King Columbia by the big Grand Coulee Dam.

Ramblin' 'Round

Words by
WOODY GUTHRIE

Music based on "Goodnight, Irene" by
HUDDIE LEDBETTER and JOHN LOMAX

My sweetheart and my parents
I left in my old home town.
I'm out to do the best I can
As I go ramblin' around, boys,
As I go ramblin' around.

Sometimes the fruit gets rotten,
Falls down on the ground.
There's a hungry mouth for every peach
As I go a-ramblin' around, boys,
As I go ramblin' around.

The peach trees they are loaded,
The limbs are bending down.
I pick 'em all day for a dollar, boys,
As I go ramblin' around, boys,
As I go ramblin' around.

I wish that I could marry;
I wish I could settle down;
But I can't save a penny, boys,
As I go ramblin' 'round.
As I go ramblin' 'round.

My mother prayed that I would be
A man of some renown;
But I am just a refugee, boys,
As I go ramblin' 'round.
As I go ramblin' 'round.

I'VE GOT TO KNOW

Words and Music by
WOODY GUTHRIE

Moderately slow, in three

UNION/LABOR

Chorus

I've got to know, yes, I've got to know, friend; Hun-gry lips ask me wher-ev-er I go! Com-rades and friends all fall-ing a-round me, I've got to know, yes, I've got to know.

Why do your war boats ride on my waters?
Why do your death bombs fall from my skies?
Why do you burn my farm and my town down?
I've got to know, friend, I've got to know! (Chorus)

What makes your boats haul death to my people?
Nitro blockbusters, big cannons and guns?
Why doesn't your ship bring food and some clothing?
I've sure got to know, folks, I've sure got to know! (Chorus)

Why can't my two hands get a good pay job?
I can still plow, plant, I can still sow!
Why did your lawbook chase me off my good land?
I'd sure like to know, friend, I've just got to know! (Chorus)

What good work did you do, sir, I'd like to ask you,
To give you my money right out of my hands?
I built your big house here to hide from my people,
Why you crave to hide so, I'd love to know! (Chorus)

You keep me in jail and you lock me in prison,
Your hospital's jammed and your crazyhouse full,
What made your cop kill my trade union worker?
You'll hafta talk plain 'cause I sure have to know! (Chorus)

Why can't I get work and cash my big paycheck?
Why can't I buy things in your place and your store?
Why do you close my plant down and starve all my buddies?
I'm asking you, sir, 'cause I've sure got to know! (Chorus)

AND DON'T COME BACK TILL YOU REGISTER TO VOTE

Dying Miner

Words and Music by
WOODY GUTHRIE

Goodbye to Dickie and Honey,
Goodbye to the wife that I love.
Lot of these men not coming home
Tonight when the work whistle blows. (Chorus)

It looks like the end for me
And all of my buddies I see,
We're all writing letters to children we love,
Please carry our word to our wives.

We found a little place in the air,
Crawled and drug ourselves here.
But the smoke is bad and the fumes coming in,
And the gas is burning my eyes. (Chorus)

Forgive me for the things I done wrong,
I love you lots more than you know.
When the night whistle blows and I don't come home,
Do all that you can to help Mom.

I can hear the moans and groans,
More than a hundred good men.
Just work and fight and try to see
That this never happens again. (Chorus)

My eyes are blinded with fumes,
But it sounds like the men are all gone
'Cept Joe Ballantini, Fred Gutzler and Joy,
Trapped down in this hellhole of fire.

Please name our new baby Joe,
So he'll grow up like big Joe.
He'll work and he'll fight and he'll fix up the mines
So fires can't kill daddies no more. (Chorus)

I took the words for this song from the "messages" written by the trapped miners on the wall of slate rock.
The incident occurred at the Centralia Mines in Illinois in 1947 WG

THE SINKING OF THE REUBEN JAMES

Words and Music by
WOODY GUTHRIE

Well, a hundred men went down in that dark watery grave;
When that good ship went down only forty-four were saved.
'Twas the last day of October we saved the forty-four
From the cold ocean waters and the cold icy shore. (Chorus)

It was there in the dark of that uncertain night
That we watched for the U-boats and waited for the fight.
Then a whine and a rock and a great explosion roared,
And laid the Reuben James on that cold ocean floor. (Chorus)

Now tonight there are lights in our country so bright –
In the farms, in the cities, they're telling of this plight.
Now our mighty battleships will steam the bounding main
And remember the name of that good Reuben James. (Chorus)

Jesus Christ

Words and Music by
WOODY GUTHRIE
(Melody based on a traditional theme)

* Chord symbols in parentheses for guitar with capo on 1st fret.

He went to the preacher, He went to the sheriff,
He told them all the same,
"Sell all of your jewelry and give it to the poor,"
And they laid Jesus Christ in His grave.

When Jesus come to town, the working folks around
Believed what He did say,
But the bankers and the preachers they nailed Him on a cross,
And they laid Jesus Christ in the grave. (Chorus)

And the people held their breath when they heard about His death,
Everybody wondered why.
It was the big landlord and the soldiers that they hired
To nail Jesus Christ in the sky.

This song it was wrote in New York City,
Of rich man, preacher and slave.
If Jesus was to preach what He preached in Galilee,
They would lay poor Jesus in His grave. (Chorus)

Tom Joad

Words and Music by
WOODY GUTHRIE

That truck rolled away in a cloud of dust,
Tommy turned his face toward home,
He met Preacher Casey and they had a little drink,
But they found that his family they was gone,
He found that his family they was gone.

He found his mother's old-fashioned shoe,
Found his daddy's hat,
And he found little Muley and Muley said:
"They've been tractored out by the cats.
They've been tractored out by the cats."

Tom Joad walked down to the neighbor's farm,
Found his family.
They took Preacher Casey and loaded in a car
And his mother said: "We've got to git away."
His mother said: "We've got to git away."

Now the twelve of the Joads made a mighty heavy load,
But Grandpa Joad did cry.
He picked up a handful of land in his hand,
Said: "I'm stayin' with the farm till I die.
Yes, I'm stayin' with my farm till I die."

They fed him short ribs and coffee and soothing syrup
And Grandpa Joad did die.
They buried Grandpa Joad by the side of the road,
Grandma on the California side.
They buried Grandma on the California side.

They stood on a mountain and they looked to the West,
And it looked like the promised land,
That bright green valley with a river running through,
There was work for every single hand, they thought.
There was work for every single hand.

The Joads rode away to the jungle camp,
There they cooked a stew,
And the hungry little kids of the jungle camp
Said: "We'd like to have some too."
Said: "We'd like to have some too."

Now a deputy sheriff fired loose at a man,
Shot a woman in the back.
Before he could take his aim again
Preacher Casey dropped him in his tracks.
Preacher Casey dropped him in his tracks.

They handcuffed Casey and they took him to jail,
And then he got away.
And he met Tom Joad on the old river bridge,
And these few words he did say, poor boy,
These few words he did say:

"I preached for the Lord a mighty long time,
Preached about the rich and the poor.
Us workin' folks is all get together
'Cause we ain't got a chance anymore,
We ain't got a chance anymore."

Now the deputies come and Tom and Casey run
To the bridge where the water run down.
But the vigilante thugs hit Casey with a club,
They laid Preacher Casey on the ground, poor Casey,
They laid Preacher Casey on the ground.

Tom Joad he grabbed that deputy's club,
Hit him over the head.
Tom Joad took flight in the dark, rainy night,
And a deputy and a preacher lying dead, two men,
A deputy and a preacher lying dead.

Tom run back where his mother was asleep,
He woke her up out of bed.
Then he kissed goodbye to the mother that he loved.
Said what Preacher Casey said, Tom Joad,
He said what Preacher Casey said.

"Ev'rybody might be just one big soul,
Well it looks that-a way to me.
Everywhere that you look in the day or night
That's where I'm gonna be, Ma,
That's where I'm gonna be."

"Wherever little children are hungry and cry,
Wherever people ain't free,
Wherever men are fightin' for their rights,
That's where I'm gonna be, Ma,
That's where I'm gonna be."

I wrote this song one night in New York. It was the night that I saw
the moving picture, *The Grapes of Wrath* by John Steinbeck. If I
could only think of the name of the friend that lived in that apartment
I would sure like to say thank you. You are friendly and wine is good.
And this is on a Victor Record.

PRETTY BOY FLOYD

Words and Music by
WOODY GUTHRIE

Moderately, in two

If you'll gath-er 'round me, chil-dren, A sto-ry I will tell 'Bout Pret-ty Boy Floyd, an out-law, Ok-la-ho-ma knew him well.____

It was in the town of Shawnee,
A Saturday afternoon,
His wife beside him in the wagon,
As into town they rode.

There a deputy sheriff approached him
In a manner rather rude,
Using vulgar words of anger,
And his wife, she overheard.

Pretty Boy grabbed a log chain,
And the deputy grabbed his gun,
In the fight that followed,
He laid that deputy down.

Then he took to the trees and timber,
Along the river shore,
Hiding on the river bottom,
And he never come back no more.

Yes, he took to the trees and timber,
To live a life of shame,
Every crime in Oklahoma
Was added to his name.

But many a starvin' farmer
The same old story told,
How the outlaw paid their mortgage
And saved their little home.

Others tell you 'bout a stranger
That comes to beg a meal,
Underneath his napkin
Left a thousand-dollar bill.

It was in Oklahoma City,
It was on a Christmas Day,
There was a whole car load of groceries,
Come with a note to say:

"Well, you say that I'm an outlaw,
You say that I'm a thief;
Here's a Christmas dinner
For the families on relief."

Yes, as through this world I've wandered,
I've seen lots of funny men,
Some will rob you with a six-gun,
And some with a fountain pen.

And as through your life you travel,
Yes, as through your life you roam,
You won't never see an outlaw
Drive a family from their home.

a libral is a feller that wood like to git his hands on somethin to give to the poore.....

DEAD OR ALIVE

Words and Music by
WOODY GUTHRIE

Well, he even sent me my picture;
Yes, he even sent me my picture;
How do I look, boys, dead or alive?
How do I look, boys, dead or alive?, (Chorus)

Well, he said he would pay expenses;
Yes, he said he would pay expenses;
Dead or alive, no thanks!
New sheriff, I'm a poor boy.

Well, he said he would feed and clothe me;
Yes, he said he would feed and clothe me;
Dead or alive, no thanks!
New sheriff, I'm a poor boy. (Chorus)

Well, I'm sorry I can't come, sheriff;
Yes, I'm sorry but I can't come, sheriff;
Dead or alive, no thanks!
New sheriff, I'm a poor boy. (Chorus)

I don't like your hard-rock hotel;
I don't like your hard-rock hotel;
Dead or alive, new sheriff;
No thanks, I'm a poor boy. (Chorus)

I gotta go down and see my little sweet thing;
Gonna go down and see my little sweet thing;
Dead or alive, yes, Lord!
No thanks, new sheriff. (Chorus)

31

East Texas Red

Words and Music by
WOODY GUTHRIE

Country waltz

Down in the scrub oak tim-bers ___ of the south-east Tex-as Gulf, There used to ride a brake-man ___ And a brake-man dou-ble tough. He worked the town of Kil-gore And Long-view nine miles down, And us trav-'lers called him "East Tex-as Red", the mean-est bull a-round. ___

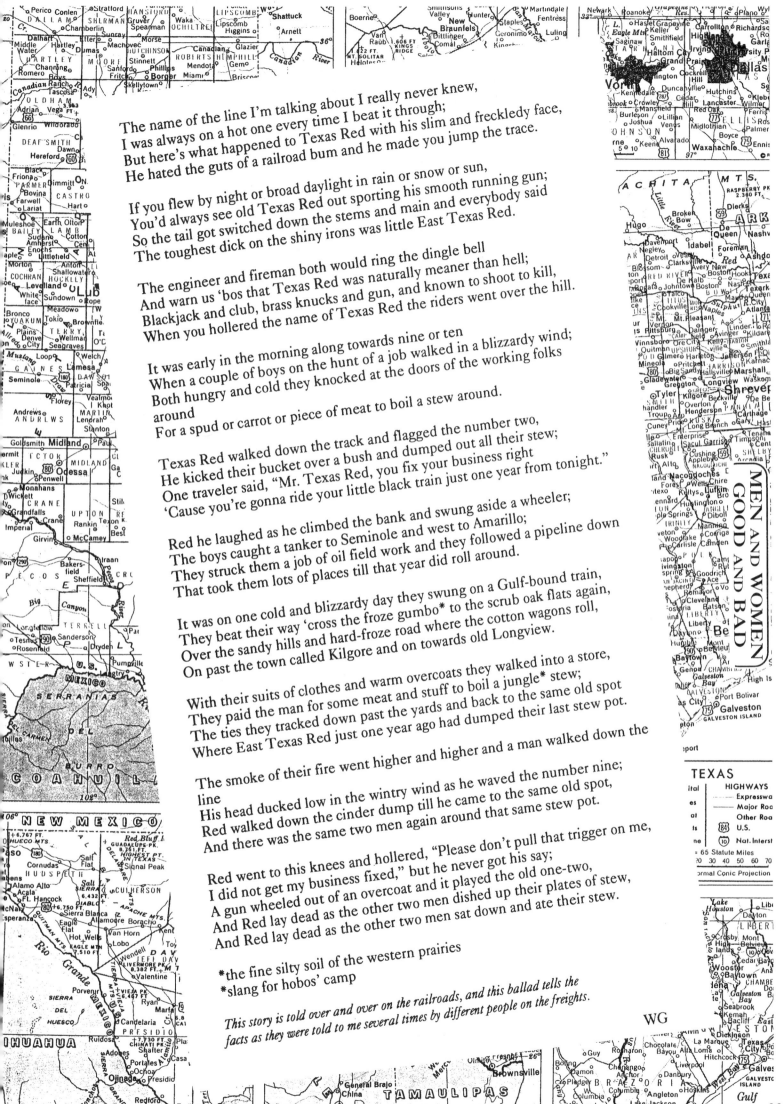

The name of the line I'm talking about I really never knew,
I was always on a hot one every time I beat it through;
But here's what happened to Texas Red with his slim and freckledy face,
He hated the guts of a railroad bum and he made you jump the trace.

If you flew by night or broad daylight in rain or snow or sun,
You'd always see old Texas Red out sporting his smooth running gun;
So the tail got switched down the stems and main and everybody said
The toughest dick on the shiny irons was little East Texas Red.

The engineer and fireman both would ring the dingle bell
And warn us 'bos that Texas Red was naturally meaner than hell;
Blackjack and club, brass knucks and gun, and known to shoot to kill,
When you hollered the name of Texas Red the riders went over the hill.

It was early in the morning along towards nine or ten
When a couple of boys on the hunt of a job walked in a blizzardy wind;
Both hungry and cold they knocked at the doors of the working folks around
For a spud or carrot or piece of meat to boil a stew around.

Texas Red walked down the track and flagged the number two,
He kicked their bucket over a bush and dumped out all their stew;
One traveler said, "Mr. Texas Red, you fix your business right
'Cause you're gonna ride your little black train just one year from tonight."

Red he laughed as he climbed the bank and swung aside a wheeler;
The boys caught a tanker to Seminole and west to Amarillo;
They struck them a job of oil field work and they followed a pipeline down
That took them lots of places till that year did roll around.

It was on one cold and blizzardy day they swung on a Gulf-bound train,
They beat their way 'cross the froze gumbo* to the scrub oak flats again,
Over the sandy hills and hard-froze road where the cotton wagons roll,
On past the town called Kilgore and on towards old Longview.

With their suits of clothes and warm overcoats they walked into a store,
They paid the man for some meat and stuff to boil a jungle* stew;
The ties they tracked down past the yards and back to the same old spot
Where East Texas Red just one year ago had dumped their last stew pot.

The smoke of their fire went higher and higher and a man walked down the line
His head ducked low in the wintry wind as he waved the number nine;
Red walked down the cinder dump till he came to the same old spot,
And there was the same two men again around that same stew pot.

Red went to this knees and hollered, "Please don't pull that trigger on me,
I did not get my business fixed," but he never got his say;
A gun wheeled out of an overcoat and it played the old one-two,
And Red lay dead as the other two men dished up their plates of stew,
And Red lay dead as the other two men sat down and ate their stew.

*the fine silty soil of the western prairies
*slang for hobos' camp

This story is told over and over on the railroads, and this ballad tells the facts as they were told to me several times by different people on the freights.

MEN AND WOMEN
GOOD AND BAD

WG

Gypsy Davy

Words and New Music Adaptation by
WOODY GUTHRIE

It was late last night when my boss come home Ask-ing a-bout his la - dy;_____ The on - ly an - swer he re - ceived: "She's gone with the Gyp - sy Da - vy, Gone with the Gyp - sy Dave."_____

Go saddle for me my buckskin horse
And a hundred dollar saddle.
Point out to me their wagon tracks
And after them I'll travel,
After them I'll ride.

Well, I had not rode 'til the midnight moon,
I saw their campfire gleaming.
I heard the notes of the big guitar
And the voice of the gypsy singing
The song of the Gypsy Dave.

It was there in the light of the camping fire
I saw her fair face beaming,
Her heart in tune to the big guitar
The song of the gypsy singing
That song of the Gypsy Dave.

"Have you forsaken your house and home?
Have you forsaken your baby?
Have you forsaken your husband dear
To go with the Gypsy Davy?
And sing with the Gypsy Davy
The song of the Gypsy Dave."

"Yes, I've forsaken my husband dear
To go with the Gypsy Davy,
And I've forsaken my mansion high
But not my blue-eyed baby,
Not my blue-eyed babe."

She smiled to leave her husband dear
And go with the Gypsy Davy;
But the tears come a-trickling down her cheeks
To think about the blue-eyed baby.
To think about the blue-eyed babe.

Take off, take off your buck-skin gloves
Made of Spanish leather;
Give to me your lily-white hand
And we'll ride home together
And home again we'll ride.

No, I won't take off my buckskin gloves,
Made of Spanish leather.
I'll go my way from day to day
And sing with the Gypsy Davy
The song of the Gypsy Dave.

PHILADELPHIA LAWYER

Words and Music by
WOODY GUTHRIE

Moderate waltz

Way out in Re - no, Ne - va - da, _____ Where the ro - man - ces
bloom and fade, _____ There was a Phil - a - del - phi - a
law - yer _____ mak-in' love to a Hol - ly - wood maid. _____

"Come, love, and we'll go rambling
Down where the lights are so bright.
I'll win you a divorce from your husband
And we can get married tonight."

While Bill was a gun-totin' cowhand,
Ten notches was carved on his gun,
And all of the boys around Reno
Left Bill's Hollywood sweetheart alone.

One night when Bill was returning
From riding the range in the cold,
He was thinking of his Hollywood sweetheart,
Her love was as lasting as gold.

As he drew near to her window,
Two shadows he saw on her shade.
Was the great Philadelphia lawyer
Makin' love to Bill's Hollywood maid.

The night was as still as the desert,
The moon hangin' high overhead.
Bill listened awhile through the window;
He could hear every word that they said:

"Your hands are so pretty and lovely,
Your form is so rare and divine.
Come, go back with me to Philadelphia
And leave this wild cowboy behind."

Now tonight back in old Pennsylvania,
Amongst her beautiful pines,
There's one less Philadelphia lawyer
In old Philadelphia tonight.

MEN AND WOMEN
GOOD AND BAD

Takin' It Easy

Moderately, in two

Words and Music by
WOODY GUTHRIE

That bigeye girl alivin' right next door
Beena tryin' ta connect for a year or more;
Practice whistle blew an' I flew downstairs.
She said, "Slow down, man!" She grabb'd a han'fulla hair. (Chorus)

Town's pitch dark, we cain't light no light;
This ole shelter hole's a lot blacker than night;
Babe O' Baby, anda Man O' Man!
Holdin' hands in th' dark! Both of us feelin' right. (Chorus)

I shook like a leaf in the wind th't blows;
Shivvered and I shimmied from my head to m'toes;
I broke in such a hot sweat I soaked my clothes;
She purred just like a kittenkat diggin' in close. (Chorus)

It may be a terrible thing ta say;
FBI might lay me in th' jail this day;
But, her perfume smell'd sa sweet alla 'round,
I'ma prayin' that all clear toot don't sound! (Chorus)

She wiggled and oozed in closer ta me;
I felt her permanent wave abrushin' my shirtsleeve;
Felt her hot breath afoggin' up against my neck;
My hand was hot enuff ta cook a hard boiled egg. (Chorus)

Yes, the All Clear blowed and we signed for peace;
We got married just as perty as ya doggone please;
Six kids we've got achasin' 'round our place;
We keep our skillet jist slick as grease. (Chorus)

If this atombomb chases you down in a hole,
If it looks too dark to suit your soul,
Just grab on tight an' give an easy squeeze;
You'll slide into Glory where they've all got peace. (Chorus)

Woman At Home

Words and Music by
WOODY GUTHRIE

Moderately

Your folk-song sing-ers all go a-round a-singing How bad are the men, how___ sin-ful are the wo-men; I got a wo-man at home ___ with her door left o-pen for me; ___ I got a wo-man at home ___ with her gate wide o-pen for me. ___

(I got a)

MEN AND WOMEN
GOOD AND BAD

These singers going round do the same old thing
Run all my women down on your slick-slidin' string
I got a woman at home with her screen left open for me
I got a woman at home with her blinds wide open for me.

You grizzly bear boys all of you fall high flyers
You're sixteen kids behind me in the passion fires
I got a woman at home with her door left open for me
I got a woman at home with her gate wide open for me.

I'm a high ballad man, I'm a folk singer too;
I sing about the good things men and women do;
I got a woman at home with her sheets left open for me;
I got a woman at home with her blanket wide open for me.

I was first born a-singin' in this big world,
Raised by the laborin' movements of a hundred pretty girls;
I got a woman at home with her arms left open for me.
I got a woman at home with her hands wide open for me.

New York Town

Moderately fast blues

Words and Music by
WOODY GUTHRIE

I was standing down in New York town one day, ____

____ Standing down in New York town one day, ____

I was standing down in New York town one

day, ____ ____ Singing hey, hey, hey, hey. ____

I was broke, I didn't have a dime... *(3 x each)*

Every good man gets a little hard luck sometimes...

Down and out and he ain't got a dime...

I'm gonna ride that new morning railroad (train)...

Standin' on my sidewalk curb today...

Holdin' my last old dollar in my hand...

Lookin' for a woman that's lookin' for a man...

If you don't want me, you don't have to stall...

I can get more women than a passenger train can haul...

If you don't want me, please just leave me be...

I can buy more lovers than the Civil War set free...

Never comin' back to this man's town again...

Talking Dust Bowl

Words and Music by
WOODY GUTHRIE

Talking blues

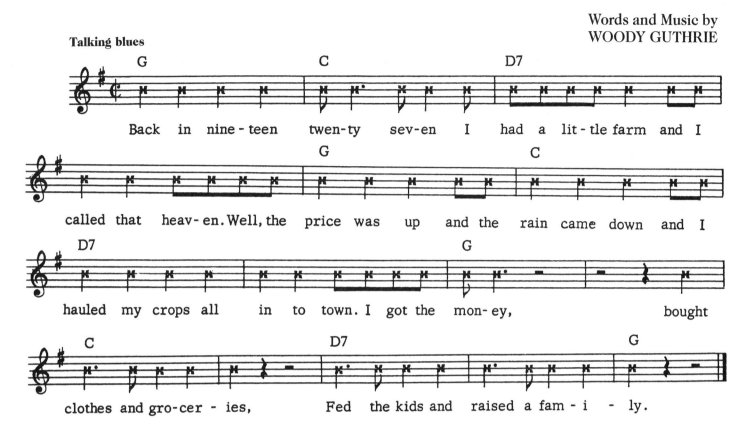

Back in nine-teen twen-ty sev-en I had a lit-tle farm and I called that heav-en. Well, the price was up and the rain came down and I hauled my crops all in to town. I got the mon-ey, bought clothes and gro-cer-ies, Fed the kids and raised a fam-i-ly.

Rain quit and the wind got high,
And a black old dust storm filled the sky,
And I swapped my farm for a Ford machine,
And I poured it full of this gasoline.
And I started - rocking and a-rolling -
Over the mountains out towards the old peach bowl.

Way up yonder on a mountain road,
I had a hot motor and a heavy load,
I was going pretty fast, I wasn't even stopping,
A-bouncing up and down like a popcorn popping.
Had a breakdown - a sort of a nervous bust-down
    of some kind.
There was a fellow there, a mechanic fellow,
    said it was engine trouble.

Way up yonder on a mountain curve,
It was way up yonder in the piney woods,
And I give that rolling Ford a shove,
And I was going to coast as far as I could.
Commenced coasting; picking up speed;
(there) was a hairpin turn; I...didn't make it.

Man alive, I'm a-telling you
The fiddles and the guitars really flew.
That Ford took off like a flying squirrel
And it flew halfway around the world
Scattered wives and childrens
All over the side of that mountain.

We got out to the West Coast broke,
So dad gum hungry I thought I'd croak,
And I bummed up a spud or two,
And my wife fixed up a 'tater stew.
We poured the kids full of it. Mighty thin stew,
    though;
You could read a magazine right through it.

Always have figured that if it had been
    just a little bit thinner some of
        these here politicians could have seen
            through it.

DUST CAN'T KILL ME.

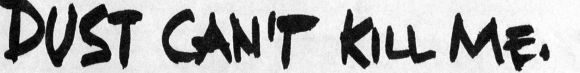

Words and Music by
WOODY GUTHRIE

That old dust storm killed my fam'ly,
But it can't kill me, Lord, and it can't kill me.

That old landlord, he got my homestead,
But he can't get me, Lord, and he can't get me.

That old dry spell killed my crop, boys,
But it can't kill me, Lord, and it can't get me.

That old tractor got my home, boys,
But it can't get me, Lord, and it can't get me.

That old tractor run my house down,
But it can't get me down, and it can't get me.

That old pawn shop got my furniture,
But it can't get me, Lord, and it can't get me.

That old highway, it's got my relatives,
But it can't get me, Lord, and it can't get me.

That old dust might kill my wheat, boys,
But it can't kill me, Lord, and it can't kill me.

I have weathered many a dust storm,
But it can't get me, boys, and it can't kill me.

That old dust storm, well, it blowed my barn down
But it can't blow me down, and it can't blow me down.

That old wind might blow this world down,
But it can't blow me down, and it can't kill me.

That old dust storm killed my baby,
But it can't kill me, Lord, and it can't kill me.

This old dust storm it's a-kickin' up cinders,
This old dust storm cuttin' down my wheat,
This old dust storm it pushed my shack down,
But it didn't get me, girl, it cain't stop me.

This old dust storm it's a-kickin' up gravel
This old dust storm she's a sight to see,
Blows so dark, dark that I cain't see daylight,
But it didn't get me, girl, it cain't stop me.

This old dust storm it's a-kickin' up hardrock,
Kickin' up loose dirt from sea to sea,
If this old dirt blinds me, I still can feel ya,
It cain't stop me.

This old dust storm it's a-diggin' my farm up,
This old dirty dust storm it's a-chokin' me.
Money man broke me and this weather might break him,
But it cain't stop me, girl, it cain't stop me.

I caught me a ride down this twisting highway
With a tough truckdriver and he says to me:
"This hard wind blows my truck plumb sideways,
"But it cain't stop me, girl, it cain't stop me."

I caught myself a ride off down a Texas freight train,
Name on the boxcar was the Santy Fee,
Old wild dust storm it stopped that freight train,
But it didn't stop me, girl, it cain't stop me.

Caught myself a good ride on a big Lincoln Zephyr,
Rolled me so dangblang fast that I couldn't see,
Dust storm cracked up that there Lincoln Zephyr,
But it didn't stop me, girl, it cain't stop me.

It blowed me out there towards Arizona (Aryyzzeenoo)
To the town of Tucson and it stranded me,
Darn nigh starved there at cotton boll gravvin',
But it didn't stop me, girl, it cain't stop me.

It blows me southwards, blows me northwards,
Blows me back westwards and blows me to the east,
It dug a Grand Canyon for to be my graveyard,
But it didn't stop me, girl, it cain't stop me.

Girly, I'm still a-blowin', I'm still a-goin',
Rumblin' and a-tumblin' right back your way,
Wild weeds that rumble and big storms that rumble
Just didn't stop me, girl, just cain't stop me.

DUST STORM DISASTER

Words and Music by
WOODY GUTHRIE

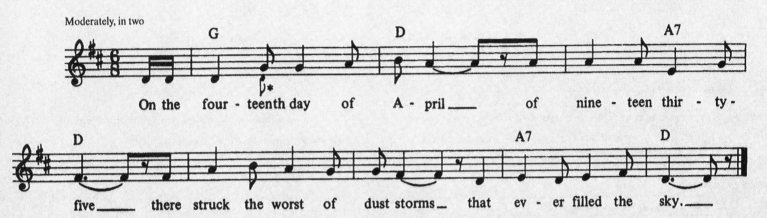

Moderately, in two

On the four-teenth day of A-pril __ of nine-teen thir-ty-

five __ there struck the worst of dust storms __ that ev-er filled the sky. __

* Sing this note on even numbered verses.

You could see that dust storm coming
The cloud looked death-like black
And through our mighty nation
It left a dreadful track.

From Oklahoma City
To the Arizona line
Dakota and Nebraska
To the lazy Rio Grande.

It fell across our city
Like a curtain of black rolled down
We thought it was our judgment
We thought it was our doom.

The radio reported
We listened with alarm
The wild and windy actions
Of this great mysterious storm.

From Albuquerque and Clovis
And old New Mexico
They said it was the blackest
That ever they had saw.

In old Dodge City, Kansas,
The dust had rung their knell,
And a few more comrades sleeping
On top of old Boot Hill.

From Denver, Colorado,
Thay said it blew so strong,
They thought that they could hold out,
They did not know how long.

Our relatives were huddled
Into their oil-boom shacks,
And the children they were crying
As it whistled through the cracks.

And the family was crowded
Into their little room,
They thought the world had ended,
And they thought it was their doom.

The storm took place at sundown.
It lasted through the night.
When we looked out next morning
We saw a terrible sight.

We saw outside our window
Where wheatfields they had grown,
Was now a rippling ocean
Of dust the wind had blown.

It covered up our fences,
It covered up our barns,
It covered up our tractors
In this wild and dusty storm.

We loaded our jalopies
And piled our families in,
We rattled down that highway
To never come back again.

DUST BOWL

I Ain't Got No Home

Words and Music by
WOODY GUTHRIE

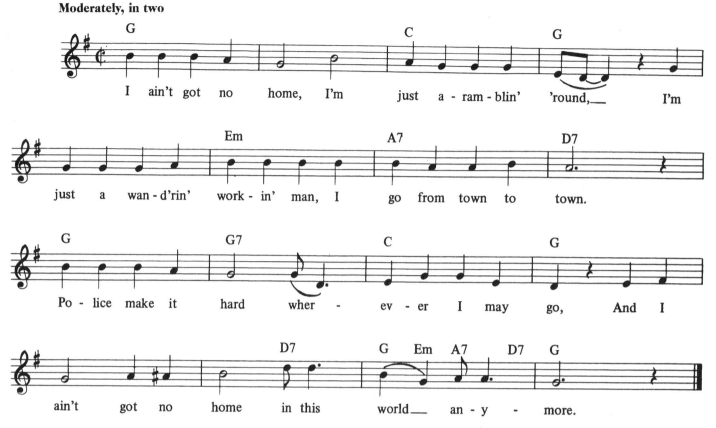

Moderately, in two

I ain't got no home, I'm just a-ram-blin' 'round,__ I'm just a wan-d'rin' work-in' man, I go from town to town. Po-lice make it hard wher-ev-er I may go, And I ain't got no home in this world__ an-y-more.

My brothers and my sisters
Are stranded on this road;
It's a hot and dusty road
That a million feet have trod.
    Rich man took my home and he drove me from my door
And I ain't got no home in this world anymore.

I was farmin' on the shares
And always I was poor;
My crops I lay
Into the banker's store.
My wife took down and died
Upon my cabin floor
    And I ain't got no home in this world anymore.

I mined in your mines
And I gathered in your corn;
I been working, mister,
Since the day that I was born.
Now I worry all the time
Like I never did before
    'Cause I ain't got no home in this world anymore.

Now as I look around
It's mighty plain to see
This wide and wicked world
Is a funny place to be.
    The gambling man is rich and the working man is poor
    And I ain't got no home in this world anymore.

ONE/THIRD OF THE PEOPLE IS INADEQUATELY HOUSED!
Prob'ly more

HARD TRAVELIN'

Words and Music by
WOODY GUTHRIE

Moderately, in two

I've been a-riding them fast rattlers, I thought you knowed,
I've been a-riding them flat wheelers way down the road,
I've been a-riding them blind passengers, dead enders, kicking up cinders,
I've been a-having some hard traveling, Lord.

I've been a-hitting some hard rock mining, I thought you knowed,
I've been a-leaning on a pressure drill way down the road,
Hammer flying, air hose sucking, six foot of mud and I sure been a-mucking,
And I've been a-hitting some hard traveling, Lord.

I've been a-hitting some hard harvesting, I thought you knowed,
North Dakota to Kansas City way down the road,
Cutting that wheat, stacking that hay, and I'm trying to make about a dollar a day,
And I've been a-having some hard traveling, Lord.

I've been a-working that Pittsburgh steel, I thought you knowed,
I've been a-dumping that red-hot slag way down the road,
I've been a-blasting, I've been a-firing, I've been a-pouring red-hot iron,
And I've been a-hitting some hard traveling, Lord.

I've been a-laying in a hard rock jail, I thought you knowed,
I've been a-laying out ninety days way down the road,
Damned old judge he said to me, "It's ninety days for vagrancy,"
And I've been a-hitting some hard traveling, Lord.

DUST BOWL

Dust Pneumonia Blues

Words and Music by
WOODY GUTHRIE

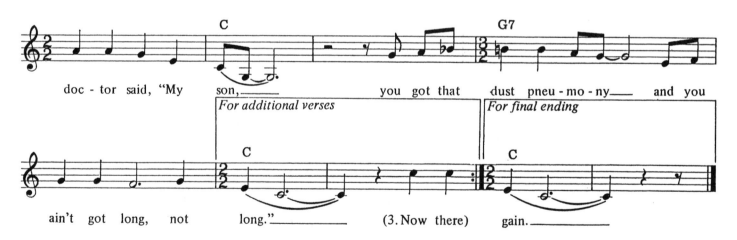

Now there ought to be some yodeling in this song,
And there ought to be some yodeling in this song,
But I can't yodel for the rattling in my lung.

My good gal sings the dust pneumony blues,
My good gal sings the dust pneumony blues,
She loves me 'cause she's got the dust pneumony too.

If it wasn't for choppin' my hoe would turn to rust,
If it wasn't for choppin' my hoe would turn to rust,
I can't find a woman in this black old Texas dust.

Down in Oklahoma the wind blows mighty strong,
Down in Oklahoma the wind blows mighty strong,
If you want to get a mama, just sing a California song.

Down in Texas my gal fainted in the rain,
Down in Texas my gal fainted in the rain
I threw a bucket of dirt in her face just to bring her back again.

WGP/TRO - © Copyright 1963 (Renewed), 1976 (Renewed) Woody Guthrie Publications, Inc. & Ludlow Music, Inc., New York, NY
Administered by Ludlow Music, Inc.
International Copyright Secured
All Rights Reserved Including Public Performance For Profit

44

Going Down the Road

(I Ain't Going to Be Treated this Way)

Words and Music by
WOODY GUTHRIE and LEE HAYS

Moderately, in two

I'm blow-in' down_ this old dust - y road; _____ Yes, I'm

blow-in' down this old dust - y road; _____ I'm

blow-in' down this old dust - y road, Lord God, And I

ain't a - gon - na be treat - ed this - a way. _____

I'm going where the water tastes like wine... *(3 x each)*

I'm going where them dust storms never blow...

They say I'm a dust bowl refugee...

I'm looking for a job at honest pay...

My children need three square meals a day...

Your two-dollar shoe hurts my feet...

Takes a ten-dollar shoe to fit my feet...

I'm going down this old dusty road...

I'm goin' down that road feelin' bad...

They got me way down in jail on my knees...

They feed me on corn bread and beans...

I'm goin' where the climate suits my clothes...

I'm goin' where the chilly winds never blow...

I'm goin' where them grapes an' peaches grow...

I'm gonna change this damned old world around...

DUST BOWL

Dust Bowl Blues

Words and Music by
WOODY GUTHRIE

1. I just blowed in and I got them dust bowl blues,____ I
2.- 9. *See Additional Lyrics*

just blowed in and I got them dust bowl blues;____ I just blowed in____

____ and I'll blow back out____ a - gain.____

9. go.____ And I just blowed in____ and I'll

soon blow out____ a - gain.____

I guess you've heard about every kind of blues
I guess you've heard about every kind of blues
But when the dust gets high
You can't even see the sky.

I've seen the dust so black that I couldn't see a thing
I've seen the dust so black that I couldn't see a thing
And the wind so cold
Boy, it nearly cut your water off.

I've seen the wind so high that it blowed my fences down
I've seen the wind so high that it blowed my fences down
Buried my tractor
Six feet underground.

Well, it turned my farm into a pile of sand
Yes, it turned my farm into a pile of sand
I had to hit that road
With a bottle in my hand.

I spent ten years down in that old dust bowl
I spent ten years down in that old dust bowl
When you get that dust pneumonia
Boy, it's a time to go.

I had a gal and she was young and sweet
I had a gal and she was young and sweet
But a dust storm buried her
Sixteen hundred feet.

She was a good gal, long, tall and stout
She was a good gal, long, tall and stout
I had to get a steam shovel
Just to dig my darlin' out.

These dusty blues are the dustiest ones I know
These dusty blues are the dustiest ones I know
Buried head over heels in the black old dust
I had to pack up and go.
And I just blowed in and I'll soon blow out again.

Dust Bowl Refugee

Words and Music by
WOODY GUTHRIE

We are ramblers so they say,
We are only here today.
Then we travel with the seasons,
We're the dust bowl refugees.

From the southland and the droughtland
Come the wife and kids and me.
And this old world is a hard world
For a dust bowl refugee.

Yes we ramble and we roam,
And the highway, that's our home.
It's a never-ending highway
For a dust bowl refugee.

Yes, we wander and we work
In your crops and in your fruit.
Like the whirlwinds on the desert,
That's the dust bowl refugees.

I'm a dust bowl refugee,
I'm a dust bowl refugee,
And I wonder will I always
Be a dust bowl refugee?

Little Seed

Words and Music by
WOODY GUTHRIE

Moderately slow, in one

The rain it come and it washed my ground
I thought my little seed was going to drown.
I waded and I splashed and I carried my seed
I planted it again on some higher ground. (Chorus)

The sun got hot and my ground got dry.
I thought my little seed would burn and die.
I carried some water from a watering mill,
I said, "Little seed, you can drink your fill." (Chorus)

The snow it blowed and the wind it blew;
My little seed grew and it grew and it grew.
It grew up a cradle all soft inside;
And a baby was sleeping there covered over with vines.

Howdi Do

Words and Music by
WOODY GUTHRIE

Bright Country feel

Verse:

I stick out my lit-tle hand to ev-'ry wo-man, kid and man and I shake it up and down, how-ji-do, how-ji-do. Yes, I shake it up and down,_ how-ji-do._____

Chorus:

How-dy doo-zle doo-dle doo-zie how-ji hi-jie hee-jie ho-jie, how-ji ho-jie hee-jie hi-jie, how-ji-do, how-ji-do, how-ji-do sir, doo-dle doo-sie, how-ji-do._____

And when you walk in my door,
I will run across my floor,
And I'll shake you by the hand,
Howjido, howjido,
Yes, I'll shake it up and down, howjido (Chorus)

On my sidewalk, on my street,
Any place that we do meet,
Then I'll shake you by your hand,
Howjido, howjido,
Yes, I'll shake it up and down, howjido (Chorus)

When I first jump out of bed,
Out my window goes my head,
And I shake it up and down,
Howjido, howjido,
I shake at all my windows, howjido.(Chorus)

I feel glad when you feel good,
You brighten up my neighborhood,
Shakin' hands with ev'rybody,
Howjido, howjido,
Shakin' hands with ev'rybody, howjido.(Chorus)

When I meet a dog or cat,
I will rubby rub his back,
Shakey, shakey, shakey paw,
Howjido, howjido,
Shaking hands with everybody, howdy do. (Chorus)

WHY, OH WHY

Country waltz

Verse

Words and Music by
WOODY GUTHRIE

Why can't a dish break a ham-mer? _____ Why, oh why, oh why? 'Cause a ham-mer's a hard head, _____ Good-bye, good-bye, _____ good-bye. _____

Chorus:

Why, oh why, oh why, oh why? Why, oh why, oh why? Be - cause, be - cause, be - cause, be - cause, _____ Good-bye, good-bye, _____ good-bye. _____

*Cathy Ann and
Marjorie Guthrie, 1947*

Why can't a bird eat an elephant?
Why, oh why, oh why?
'Cause an elephant's got a pretty hard skin.
Goodbye, goodbye, goodbye.

Why can't a mouse eat a street car?
Why, oh why, oh why?
'Cause a mouse's stomach could never get big
  enough to hold a street car.
Goodbye, goodbye, goodbye.

Why does a horn make music?
Why, oh why, oh why?
Because the horn blower blows it.
Goodbye, goodbye, goodbye.

Why does a cow drink water?
Tell me, why, oh why?
Because a cow gets thirsty just like you
  and me and anybody else.
Goodbye, goodbye, goodbye. (Chorus)

Why don't you answer my question
Why, oh why, oh why?
'Cause I don't know the answer.
Goodbye, goodbye, goodbye.

What makes the landlord take money?
Why, oh why, oh why?
I don't know that one myself.
Goodbye, goodbye, goodbye.

Why's there no pennies for ice cream?
Why, oh why, oh why?
You put all the pennies in the telephone.
Goodbye, goodbye, goodbye.

Why can't a rabbit chase an eagle?
Tell me, why, oh why?
'Cause the last rabbit that took and chased off
  after an eagle didn't come off so good, and
  that's why rabbits don't chase eagles, and
  that's all I know about rabbits and eagles.
Because, because, because.

Why ain't my grandpa my grandma?
Why, oh why, oh why?
Same reason your dad is not your mommy.
Goodbye, goodbye, goodbye.

Why couldn't the wind blow backwards?
Why, oh why, oh why?
'Cause it might backfire and hurt somebody and if
  it hurt somebody it'd keep on hurting them.
Goodbye, goodbye, goodbye. (Chorus)

Cleano

Words and Music by
WOODY GUTHRIE

Daddy, oh Daddy, come fix my shoe,
Fix my shoe, come fix my shoe.
Daddy, oh Daddy, come fix my shoe,
And polish it nice and cleano.

Sister, oh Sister, come bathe my back,
Bathe my back, come bathe my back.
Sister, oh Sister, come bathe my back,
And make it nice and cleano.

Cleano clean, yes, cleano clean,
Cleano clean, yes, cleano clean.
Scrubbity scrubbity and rubby-dub dubbity;
And make me nice and cleano.

Brother, oh Brother, come wash my hair,
Wash my hair, come wash my hair.
Brother, oh Brother, come wash my hair,
And make it nice and cleano.

Granny, oh Granny, come wash my feet,
Wash my feet, come wash my feet.
Granny, oh Granny, come wash my feet,
And make them nice and cleano.

Sweetie, oh Sweetie, come smell-a me now,
Smell-a me now, come smell-a me now.
Sweetie, oh Sweetie, come smell-a me now,
Don't I smell nice and cleano?

MAIL MYSELF TO YOU

Brightly

Chorus:

Words and Music by
WOODY GUTHRIE

When you see me in your mail box,
Cut the string and let me out;
Wash the glue off my fingers,
Stick some bubble-gum in my mouth.

Take me out of my wrapping paper,
Wash the stamps off my head;
Pour me full of ice cream sodies,
Put me in my nice warm bed.

Cathy Ann Guthrie

Jig Along Home

Words and Music by
WOODY GUTHRIE

Centipede danced with the big giraffe,
Spider danced with the rattlesnake,
Elephant danced with the scorpio,
Jig along, jig along, jig along home. (Chorus)

Fishing worm done the fishing reel,
Lobster danced on the peacock's tail,
Baboon danced with the rising moon,
Jig along, jig along, jig along home. (Chorus)

And the rooster cut his weevily wheat,
The catfish tromped the cuckoo's feet,
The ostrich stomped with the kangaroo,
Jig along, jig along, jig along home. (Chorus)

Mama rat took off her hat,
Shook the house with the old tom cat,
The alligator beat his tail on the drum,
Jig along, jig along, jig along home. (Chorus)

The boards did rattle and the house did shake,
The clouds did laugh and the world did quake,
New moon rattled some silver spoons,
Jig along, jig along, jig along home. (Chorus)

The nails flew loose and the floors broke down,
Everybody danced around and around,
The house come down and the crowd went home,
Jig along, jig along, jig along home. (Chorus)

Put Your Finger in the Air

Words and Music by
WOODY GUTHRIE

Brightly

Put your fin-ger in the air,__ in the air; Put your fin-ger in the

air, in the air; Put your fin-ger in the air__ and

leave it a-bout a year,__ Put your fin-ger in the air,__ in the air.

Put your finger on your head, on your head;
Put your finger on your head, on your head;
Put your finger on your head.
Tell me, is it green or red?
Put your finger on your head, on your head.

Put your finger on your nose, on your nose;
Put your finger on your nose, on your nose;
Put your finger on your nose
And feel the cold wind blow;
Put your finger on your nose, on your nose.

Put your finger on your shoe, on your shoe;
Put your finger on your shoe, on your shoe;
Put your finger on your shoe
And leave it a day or two;
Put your finger on your shoe, on your shoe.

Put your finger on your chin, on your chin;
Put your finger on your chin, on your chin;
Put your finger on your chin –
That's where the food slips in;
Put your finger on your chin, on your chin.

Put your finger on your cheek, on your cheek;
Put your finger on your cheek, on your cheek;
Put your finger on your cheek
And leave it about a week;
Put your finger on your cheek, on your cheek.

Put your finger on your finger, on your finger;
Put your finger on your finger, on your finger;
Put your finger on your finger,
On your finger, on your finger;
Put your finger on your finger, on your finger.

Put your fingers all together, all together;
Put your fingers all together, all together;
Put your fingers all together
And we'll clap for better weather;
Put your fingers all together, all together.

All Work Together

Words and Music by
WOODY GUTHRIE

My sister told me,
Brother told me, too,
Lots an' lotsa work
That I can do.
I can bring her candy.
Bring him gum.
But if we all work together
Hadn't oughtta take long. So
(Chorus)

My daddy said,
And my grandpaw, too,
There's work, worka, work
For me to do.
I can paint my fence.
Mow my lawn.
But if we all work together,
Well, it shouldn't take long. So
(Chorus)

I tell Mama an' Daddy,
Grampaw an' Granmaw, too,
I tell my sister an' my brother,
Lotsa work for you to do.
You can bring me pennies
And candy and gum;
But if we all work together
'Twon't take so very long. And so
(Chorus)

Bling-Blang

Words and Music by
WOODY GUTHRIE

With a lilt
Verse:

You get a ham-mer and I'll get a nail; You catch a bird and

I'll catch a snail; You bring a board and I'll bring a saw, and

Chorus:

we'll build a house for the ba - by - o. Bling blang,

ham-mer with my ham-mer, zing - o zang - o, cut-ting with my saw.

I'll grab some mud and you grab some clay
So when it rains it won't wash away.
We'll build a house that'll be so strong,
The winds will sing my baby a song.
(Chorus)

Run bring rocks and I'll bring bricks.
A nice pretty house we'll build and fix.
We'll jump inside when the cold wind blows
And kiss our pretty little baby-o.
(Chorus)

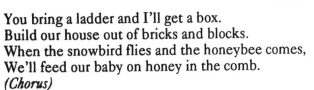

You bring a ladder and I'll get a box.
Build our house out of bricks and blocks.
When the snowbird flies and the honeybee comes,
We'll feed our baby on honey in the comb.
(Chorus)

KIDS' SONGS

My Daddy

(Flies a Ship in the Sky)

Words and Music by
WOODY GUTHRIE

A pug-nosed kid as he kicked up his heels
Said, "My daddy works in the iron and the steel.
My daddy makes planes so they fly through the sky,
That's what keeps your daddy up there so high."

    That's what keeps your daddy up there so high. (2)
    You're not afraid, well, neither am I
    'Cause my daddy keeps your daddy up there so high.

Then a shy little girl pinched her toe in the sand,
Said, "My daddy works at the place where they land.
So you tell your mama don't be afraid,
My dad'll bring your daddy back home again."

    My dad'll bring your daddy back home again. (2)
    Don't be afraid if it gets dark and rains
    'Cause my dad'll bring your daddy back home again.

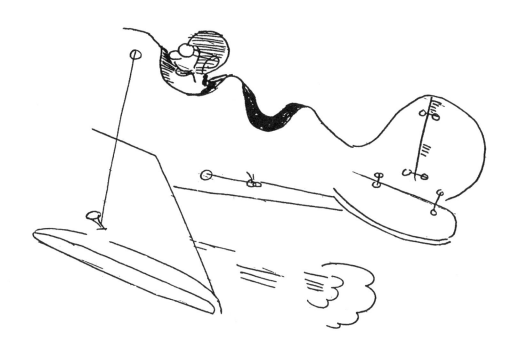

Riding In My Car

Words and Music by
WOODY GUTHRIE

Moderately, with humor

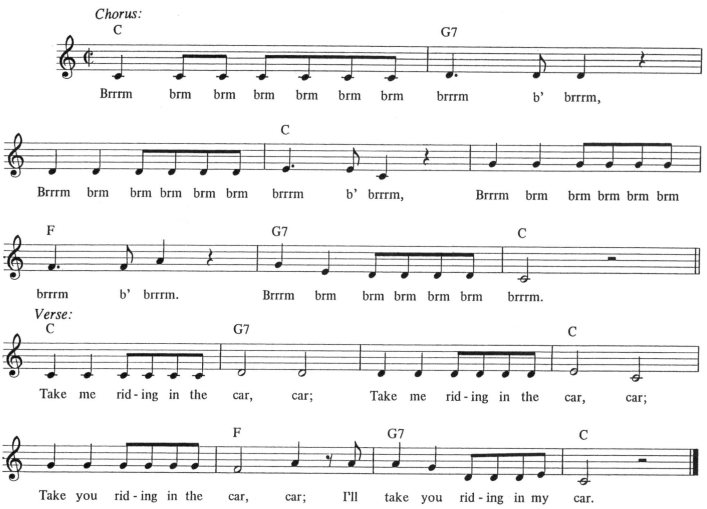

Chorus:

Brrrm brm brm brm brm brm brm brrrm b' brrrm,

Brrrm brm brm brm brm brm brrrm b' brrrm, Brrrm brm brm brm brm brm

brrrm b' brrrm. Brrrm brm brm brm brm brm brrrm.

Verse:

Take me rid-ing in the car, car; Take me rid-ing in the car, car;

Take you rid-ing in the car, car; I'll take you rid-ing in my car.

Click, clack, open up the door, girls;
Click, clack, open up the door, boys;
Front door, back door, clickety clack,
I'll take you riding in my car.

Climb, climb, rattle on the front seat;
Spree I spraddle on the back seat;
I turn my key, I step on the starter,
I'll take you riding in my car.

Engine it goes brmmm brmmm;
Engine it goes brmmm brmmm;
Front seat, back seat, boys and girls,
Take you riding in my car.

I TELL YOU JOHN
3 OF THEM ARE
MISSING!

I'm gonna take you home again;
I'm gonna zoom you home again;
Brmm brummm brummmm,
We're rolling home,
I'll take you home in my car.

Trees and houses walk along;
Trees and houses walk along;
A truck and a car and a garbage can,
Take you riding in my car.

Ships and little boats chug along;
Ships and little boats chug along;
Chug chugga chug, chuggy chug chug,
Take you riding in my car.

I'm gonna let you blow the horn;
I'm gonna let you blow the horn;
Honk honk honk and beep beep beep,
Take you riding in my car.

Grassey Grass Grass
(Grow, Grow, Grow)

Words and Music by
WOODY GUTHRIE

Films

1913 Massacre, Dreamland Productions, 2011
A Vision Shared: Tribute to Woody Guthrie & Leadbelly, Ginger Group Productions, 1988, 1991
Bound For Glory, United Artists, 1976
Man In The Sand (The Making of "Mermaid Avenue"), Rykovision ,2001
Roll On Columbia, Woody Guthrie & The Bonneville Power Administration, University of Oregon, 2000
Woody at 100! Live at the Kennedy Center, Jim Brown Productions, 2013
Woody Guthrie, Ain't Got No Home, PBS American Masters Documentary, 2007
Woody Guthrie: This Machine Kills Fascists, Snapper UK Documentary, 2005

Selected Books

Brower, Steven and Guthrie, Nora	2005 *Woody Guthrie: Artworks.* Rizzoli.
Buehler, Phillip/Guthrie, Nora/Brower, Steven	2013 *Woody Guthrie's Wardy Forty: Greystone Park State Hospital Revisited.* Woody Guthrie Publications.
	2013 *Woody Guthrie's Wardy Forty: The Interviews.* Woody Guthrie Publications.
Christensen, Bonnie	2001 *Woody Guthrie: Poet of the People.* Alfred A. Knopf.
Cohen, Ronald D.	2012 *Woody Guthrie Writing America's Songs.* Routledge.
Cray, Ed	2005 *Ramblin' Man: The Life and Times of Woody Guthrie.* W. W. Norton.
Garman, Bryan K.	2000 *A Race of Singers.* University of North Carolina Press.
Guthrie, Nora & the Woody Guthrie Archive	2012 *My Name Is New York: Ramblin' Around Woody Guthrie's Town.* PowerHouse Books.
	2014 *My Name Is New York: Ramblin' Around Woody Guthrie's Town (AudioBook).* Woody Guthrie Publications.
Guthrie, Woody	1943 *Bound for Glory.* E. P. Dutton.
	2012 *Every 100 Years: Woody Guthrie Centennial Songbook.* TRO Ludlow
	2013 *House of Earth.* Infinitum Nihil/HarperCollins.
	2014 *Woody Guthrie For Ukulele.* TRO Ludlow
Guthrie, Woody and Frazee, Maria	2004 *New Baby Train.* Little, Brown.
Guthrie, Woody and Horowitz, Dave	2014 *Honeyky Hanukah.* Random House Kids.
Guthrie, Woody and Jakobsen, Kathy	1998 *This Land Is Your Land.* Little, Brown.
Guthrie, Woody and Scott Menchin	2012 *Riding In My Car. Little,* Brown Kids.
Guthrie, Woody and Radunsky, Vladimir	2000 *Bling Blang.* Candlewick.
	2000 *Howdi Do.* Candlewick.
	2001 *My Dolly.* Candlewick.
Jackson, Mark Allan	2008 *Prophet Singer: The Voice and Vision of Woody Guthrie.* University Press of Mississippi.
Kaufman, Will	2011 *Woody Guthrie: American Radical.* Illinois University Press.
Klein, Joe	1980 Woody Guthrie: A Life. Delta.
Lomax, Alan-Guthrie, Woody-Seeger, Pete	1967, 1999, 2012 *Hard Hitting Songs For Hard-Hit People.* University of Nebraska Press.
Nowlin, Bill	2013 *Woody Guthrie American Radical Patriot.* Rounder.
Partington, John S.	2011 The Life, Music and Thought of Woody Guthrie. Ashgate.
Partridge, Elizabeth	2002 *This Land Was Made For You And Me: The Life and Songs of Woody Guthrie.* Viking Juvenile.
Santelli, Robert	2012 *This Land Is Your Land: Journey of an American Folksong.* Running Press.
Santelli, Robert and Davidson, Emily	1999 *Hard Travelin': The Life and Legacy of Woody Guthrie.* Wesleyan University Press.

Recordings by Woody Guthrie

Asch Recordings, Vols. 1-4 (Smithsonian Folkways- each CD available separately, 1999)
Ballads of Sacco and Vanzetti (Smithsonian Folkways, 1992)
Columbia River Collection (Rounder, 1988)
Dust Bowl Ballads (BMG Int'l, 1999)
Folkways: The Original Vision (Smithsonian Folkways, 1992)
The Live Wire: Woody Guthrie in Performance 1949 (Woody Guthrie Publications, 2007/Rounder, 2010)
Long Ways to Travel (Smithsonian Folkways, 1996)
My Dusty Road, Vols. 1-4 (Rounder, 2009)
Nursery Days (Smithsonian Folkways, 1992)
Songs to Grow On for Mother and Child (Smithsonian Folkways, 1992)
Struggle (Smithsonian Folkways, 1992)
Woody at 100 (Smithsonian Folkways, 2012)
Woody Guthrie American Radical Patriot-with complete Library of Congress recordings (Rounder, 2013)
Woody Guthrie Sings Folk Songs (Smithsonian Folkways, 1992)

Woody Guthrie Albums by Other Artists

Arlo Guthrie & The Guthrie Family: 20 Grow Big Songs; Here Come the Kids (Rising Son, 1992, 2014)
Arlo Guthrie with The Dillards: 32 Cents, Postage Due (Rising Son, 2008)
Arlo Guthrie & Wenzel: Every 100 Years (Indigo, 2010)
Cisco Houston: The Folkways Years (Smithsonian Folkways, 1994); Best of the Vanguard Years,2000
Country Joe McDonald: Tribute to Woody Guthrie (Rag Baby, 2008)
Elizabeth Mitchell: Little Seed (Smithsonian Folkways, 2013)
Joel Rafael: The Songs of Woody Guthrie (Inside, 2009)
James Talley: Woody Guthrie and Songs of My Oklahoma Home (Cimarron, 2000)
Vanaver Caravan: Pastures of Plenty (Coming Together Festival Productions, 2000)
Various Artists: Daddy-O-Daddy, Rare Family Songs of Woody Guthrie (Rounder, 2001)
Various Artists: Hard Travelin' film soundtrack (Rising Son, 2000)
Various Artists: Pete Remembers Woody (Appleseed, 2012)
Various Artists: Ribbon of Highway, Endless Skyway (Music Road, 2008)
Various Artists: 'Til We Outnumber 'Em (Righteous Babe, 1996)
Various Artists: A Tribute to Woody Guthrie, Carnegie Hall 1968, Hollywood Bowl 1970 (Warner, 1976)
Various Artists: Woody At 100! Live at the Kennedy Center (Sony , 2012)

New collections from the Woody Guthrie Archives

Billy Bragg & Wilco: Mermaid Avenue; Mermaid Avenue, Vol. II; Complete Sessions (Nonesuch, 1998, 2000, 2012)
David Amram with the Colorado Symphony Orchestra: This Land (Newport Classic, 2015)
Jay Farrar, Will Johnson, Anders Parker, Yim Yames: New Multitudes (Rounder, 2012)
Jonatha Brooke: The Works (Bad Dog, 2008)
Nora Guthrie: My Name Is New York: Ramblin' Around Woody Guthrie's Town (Woody Guthrie Publications, 2014)
Rob Wasserman and Friends: Note of Hope (429 Records, 2011)
The Klezmatics: Happy Joyous Hanukkah; Wonder Wheel (Jewish Music Group, 2005, 2006)
Wenzel: Ticky Tock (Contraer Musik, 2003)

INDEX